I0455416

February 2013

DEFENSE BUSINESS TRANSFORMATION

Improvements Made but Additional Steps Needed to Strengthen Strategic Planning and Assess Progress

GAO

Accountability ★ Integrity ★ Reliability

Highlights of GAO-13-267, a report to congressional committees

Improvements Made but Additional Steps Needed to Strengthen Strategic Planning and Assess Progress

Why GAO Did This Study

DOD spends billions of dollars each year to maintain key business operations intended to support the warfighter. In 2005, GAO identified DOD's approach to business transformation as high-risk because DOD had not established management responsibility, accountability, and control over business transformation-related activities and resources, and it lacked a plan with specific goals, measures, and mechanisms to monitor progress. GAO previously reported that DOD has taken steps to develop a management approach. This report addresses DOD's progress in (1) incorporating key strategic planning elements into its transformation plan; and (2) developing and implementing an approach for assessing DOD-wide progress toward business goals. GAO analyzed relevant DOD documents, reviewed prior and ongoing GAO work; and interviewed DOD officials.

What GAO Recommends

GAO recommends that DOD add information to its SMP, such as a description of key challenges and context for why goals were chosen. GAO also recommends that DOD further define its performance management approach. DOD partially concurred with our first recommendation and concurred with our second recommendation. DOD stated that it would add information to the SMP as appropriate, and continue to improve and institutionalize DBC operations. As part of these efforts, GAO believes that DOD needs to identify specific steps it will take to integrate and regularly review performance data from various sources to assess progress towards its business goals.

View GAO-13-267. For more information, contact Sharon Pickup at 202-512-9619 or pickups@gao.gov.

What GAO Found

The Department of Defense (DOD) has improved its Strategic Management Plan (SMP) by including additional strategic planning elements that were lacking from previous plans; however, the fiscal year 2012-2013 SMP still needs to incorporate some key information that would make it more useful for DOD decision makers as a guide for implementing business transformation efforts and for measuring progress. Improvements in the SMP include links between its business goals and DOD-wide goals, as well as milestone or target data that would enable DOD to better measure performance and assess progress in achieving SMP goals. However, the SMP does not fully describe the specific challenges the goals are intended to address and what the root causes of those challenges are. For example, the SMP states that the goal on strengthening DOD's acquisition processes is aimed at obtaining greater efficiency and productivity in defense spending, but the accompanying narrative does not describe what is causing acquisition-related cost growth and how the goal's initiatives may address those causes. The SMP also lacks sufficient context for why business goals and strategies were chosen or changed from prior plans, such as whether sufficient progress had been made to warrant their removal. Also, the SMP includes performance measures that do not fully reflect core activities needed to assess progress for some business goals. For example, the SMP identifies measures related to planning for contractor support, but does not address other core activities such as those related to providing contractor oversight. Refining the SMP to include this key information could help DOD better prioritize and target its reform efforts to address the underlying causes of its systemic business challenges and to achieve results.

DOD has broadly outlined a performance management approach for monitoring business transformation efforts, but has not used its governance structures to regularly review performance results or defined how these structures will routinely integrate various sources of performance data to assess department-wide progress. DOD has established governance structures to help monitor progress, such as the Defense Business Council (DBC), established in June 2012 to, among other things, review performance results to track progress against goals. However, the DBC has not regularly reviewed performance data and when reviews did occur, it did not have sufficient information to assess progress. For example, as of December 2012, the DBC had reviewed performance results only twice, and this information did not include data on all SMP measures, nor did it disclose the reasons why certain measures were at risk of missing quarterly targets. Also, these results provide only a partial picture of performance for any given business area. For example, for the area of operational energy efficiency, the SMP measures reviewed by the DBC covered only progress in reducing consumption, but not measures related to supply and security, which are key areas in DOD's strategy for achieving operational energy efficiency. Better defining and implementing a more integrated approach to reviewing performance, such as including a broader range of performance information, will enhance DOD's ability to assess progress toward its business goals.

Contents

Abbreviations

CMO	Chief Management Officer
DBC	Defense Business Council
DCMO	Deputy Chief Management Officer
DMAG	Deputy's Management Action Group
DOD	Department of Defense
GPRA	Government Performance and Results Act
QDR	Quadrennial Defense Review
SMP	Strategic Management Plan

February 12, 2013

Congressional Committees

The Department of Defense (DOD) spends billions of dollars each year to maintain key business operations intended to support the warfighter, including systems and processes related to the management of contracts, finances, the supply chain, support infrastructure, and weapon systems acquisition. We have designated a number of these areas as high risk because of their vulnerability to fraud, waste, abuse, and mismanagement and because of opportunities to achieve greater efficiencies and free up resources for higher-priority needs.[1]

In 2005, we identified DOD's approach to business transformation as a high-risk area because (1) DOD had not established clear and specific management responsibility, accountability, and control over business transformation—related activities and applicable resources; and (2) DOD lacked a clear strategic and integrated plan for business transformation with specific goals, measures, and accountability mechanisms to monitor progress.[2] Given the complexity and magnitude of the challenges facing DOD in improving business operations,[3] we reported the need for a chief management officer (CMO) with significant authority and experience to focus the necessary attention and sustain progress. We also recommended that DOD develop a comprehensive, integrated, and enterprise-wide transformation plan, supported by a strategic planning process.

Since 2005, both DOD and Congress have taken various actions to address DOD's management of business transformation efforts. For example, in May 2007, DOD designated the Deputy Secretary of Defense as the CMO for DOD. Moreover, in the National Defense Authorization

---

[1]GAO, *High-Risk Series: An Update*, GAO-11-278 (Washington, D.C.: February 2011).

[2]GAO, *High-Risk Series: An Update*, GAO-05-207 (Washington, D.C.: January 2005).

[3]According to DOD Directive 5105.82, DOD defines its business operations as the policies, processes, information, and systems relating to the end-to-end financial, logistical, facility management, human capital, acquisition, administrative, and other such functions of the DOD that support the warfighter.

Acts for Fiscal Year 2008[4] and Fiscal Year 2009,[5] Congress took steps that included

- codifying the Deputy Secretary of Defense as the CMO for DOD,

- creating a deputy chief management officer (DCMO) position,

- requiring the secretaries of the military departments to designate the department under secretaries as CMOs,

- requiring DOD to develop a strategic management plan (SMP), and

- requiring the secretary of each military department to establish a business transformation office and to develop business transformation plans.

Since 2005, we have reported periodically on DOD's progress in implementing its management approach and developing a strategic plan for business transformation. For example, in January 2011, we reported that DOD had taken positive steps, including filling key positions, such as the DCMO and military department CMOs, and establishing governance structures, but had made limited progress in its strategic planning efforts. Specifically, in its 2009 update, DOD improved its initial SMP issued in 2008, by identifying business priorities, but the plan still lacked several key elements such as including some measurable goals and funding priorities. We also reported that DOD was in the early stages of collecting performance data and had described a strategic planning process in its 2009 plan update, but had still not set up internal mechanisms to implement this process.[6]

Since we last reported in January 2011, DOD issued another update to its plan, dated September 2011, which covers fiscal years 2012-2013. We

---

[4]Pub. L. No. 110-181, § 904 (2008).

[5]Pub. L. No. 110-417, §§ 904, 908 (2008).

[6]See GAO, *Defense Business Transformation: DOD Needs to Take Additional Actions to Further Define Key Management Roles, Develop Measurable Goals, and Align Planning Efforts*, GAO-11-181R (Washington, D.C.: Jan. 26, 2011); and *Defense Business Transformation: Status of Department of Defense Efforts to Develop a Management Approach to Guide Business Transformation*, GAO-09-272R (Washington, D.C.: Jan. 9, 2009).

performed this review under the authority of the Comptroller General to conduct evaluations on his own initiative. Our objectives for this report were to assess the extent to which DOD has taken additional steps to (1) incorporate key strategic planning elements into its business transformation plan; and (2) develop and implement an approach for assessing progress on a department-wide basis toward business transformation goals.

To assess what additional steps DOD has taken to incorporate key strategic planning elements into its business transformation plan, we reviewed and analyzed relevant documents, such as DOD's current Strategic Management Plan for fiscal year 2012-2013 and prior versions; DOD's annual performance plans for fiscal years 2011 to 2013; and relevant DOD directives and memos. We assessed whether the fiscal year 2012-2013 Strategic Management Plan included key elements that we have previously identified as needed for effective strategic planning. We also relied on prior and ongoing work we have conducted in individual DOD business areas in order to assess the extent to which the plan addresses key business-related challenges. To assess the extent to which DOD has developed an approach for assessing department-wide progress toward business transformation goals, we reviewed relevant documents and interviewed senior DOD officials about the department's performance assessment approach and its related governance mechanisms for monitoring business transformation progress. For example, we reviewed DOD's Strategic Management Plans; quarterly performance results; memorandums; directives; meeting agendas; and briefing documents. We evaluated the department's performance assessment approach in light of roles and responsibilities laid out in DOD's 2009 Strategic Management Plan and in the Government Performance and Results Act of 1993, as amended,[7] and in light of key practices in results-oriented management, as identified in our previous work. For both objectives, we interviewed the Deputy Secretary of Defense, the DOD DCMO, the military department CMOs and DCMOs; and officials from the offices of several Under Secretaries of Defense and business transformation offices within the military departments to obtain their perspectives on DOD's efforts to further refine its plan and performance management approach and to achieve progress toward business transformation goals.

---

[7]The Government Performance and Results Act of 1993 (GPRA), Pub. L. No. 103-62 (1993), as recently amended by the Government Performance and Results Modernization Act of 2010, Pub. L. No. 111-352 (2011). The relevant portions of GPRA, for purposes of this report, are codified in Title 31 of the United States Code.

We conducted this performance audit from February 2012 to February 2013 in accordance with generally accepted government auditing standards. Those standards require that we plan and perform the audit to obtain sufficient, appropriate evidence to provide a reasonable basis for our findings and conclusions based on our audit objectives. We believe that the evidence obtained provides a reasonable basis for our findings and conclusions based on our audit objectives. We discuss our scope and methodology in more detail in appendix I.

Background

Since the designation of DOD's approach to business transformation as a high-risk area in 2005, we have issued several reports that discuss the development of this approach and highlight key areas for improvement, particularly in the areas of strategic planning and performance management. With regard to strategic planning, our prior work has shown that implementing significant organizational change—such as DOD is attempting to do with business transformation—requires a comprehensive, integrated strategic plan that sets a clear direction and contains key elements, such as measurable performance goals and objectives, funding priorities that are linked to goals, and aligning of goals and measures with department-wide goals and cascading goals and measures to lower organizational levels.[8] We have periodically reported on DOD's progress in incorporating these elements into its Strategic Management Plan (SMP) and highlighted key areas for improvement. Specifically, in January 2009, we reported that DOD issued its first SMP in July 2008; however, the plan did not identify specific business areas, strategic goals, objectives, or performance measures.[9] In January 2011, we reported that DOD updated its initial SMP in 2009.[10] DOD's 2009 SMP identified priorities and reform initiatives but lacked several key elements, such as a description of the problems to be addressed, some measurable goals, and funding priorities. Accordingly, we recommended, in revising its SMP, that DOD ensure that the plan contains measurable goals and funding priorities linked to those goals. DOD concurred with our recommendation.

---

[8]GAO, *Military Training: DOD Needs a Strategic Plan and Better Inventory and Requirements Data to Guide Development of Language Skills and Regional Proficiency*, GAO-09-568 (Washington, D.C.: June 19, 2009); and GAO-11-181R.

[9]GAO-09-272R.

[10]GAO-11-181R.

With regard to developing a performance management approach to measure progress, we have identified several key management practices regarding the effective use of performance information. Specifically, we found that the full benefit of collecting performance information — improved decision making and results— is only fully realized when this information is used to support management planning and decision-making functions.[11] In January 2009, we reported on DOD's continued progress in implementing its management framework for monitoring business transformation.[12] We noted, for example, that DOD had issued directives broadly defining the responsibilities of the CMO and DCMO, established an office of the DCMO, designated an Assistant DCMO, established governance structures, and named CMOs or acting CMOs in the military departments. However, DOD had still not clearly defined the authority, roles, and relationships for some entities and positions, including the unique and shared responsibilities of various governance structures for monitoring business transformation progress, as well as decision-making authority for the DCMO, and the relationship between DOD's DCMO and the military department CMOs.

In January 2011, we reported on additional steps DOD had taken to strengthen its management approach to monitoring business transformation.[13] For example, DOD filled key positions, such as the DCMO and military department CMOs; established entities, such as a governance board to identify business process improvements; and undertook various activities, such as issuing an updated SMP in July 2009, and announcing in May 2010 a department-wide effort to reduce overhead costs. We reported that DOD was in the early stages of measuring progress, and that, DOD had not set up internal mechanisms, such as procedures and milestones, by which it could reach consensus with the military departments and others on priorities, synchronize the development of plans with each other and the budget process, and guide efforts to monitor progress and take corrective action. Therefore, we recommended

---

[11]GAO, *Results-Oriented Management: Strengthening Key Practices at FEMA and Interior Could Promote Greater Use of Performance Information,* GAO-09-676 (Washington, D.C. Aug. 17, 2009); and *Managing for Results: Enhancing Agency Use of Performance Information for Management Decision Making,* GAO-05-927 (Washington, D.C.: Sept. 9, 2005).

[12]GAO-09-272R.

[13]GAO-11-181R.

that DOD issue guidance to set up a strategic planning process with such internal mechanisms. DOD partially concurred with our recommendation, stating that the department was focused on using its existing governance bodies and planning cycles to accomplish these goals.

DOD'S Business Transformation Plan Has Improved but Still Lacks Some Key Information

DOD has improved its SMP by including additional strategic planning elements previously recommended by GAO, but the SMP still lacks some key information that would make it more useful for DOD decision makers as a guide for targeting and implementing business transformation efforts, measuring progress, and positioning the department to achieve results in addressing longstanding business challenges.

DOD's Fiscal Year 2012-2013 SMP Reflects an Improvement over Previous SMPs

In September 2011, DOD issued its fourth update to the SMP for fiscal years 2012 and 2013. This plan identifies seven overarching business goals, as shown in table 1.

Table 1: Business Goals from DOD's Fiscal Year 2012-2013 Strategic Management Plan (SMP)

Goal 1	Strengthen and right-size the DOD total workforce mix (military, civilian, and contracted support) to accomplish the DOD mission and sustain superior performance in a time of constrained resources
Goal 2	Strengthen DOD financial management to respond to warfighter needs and sustain public confidence through auditable financial statements
Goal 3	Build agile and secure information technology capabilities to enhance combat power and decision-making while optimizing value
Goal 4	Increase the buying power of the DOD acquisition system and processes, spanning requirements determination, development, procurement, and support to ensure that the force structure is modernized, recapitalized, and sustained within available resources
Goal 5	Increase operational and installation energy efficiency to lower risks to our warfighters, reduce costs, and improve energy security
Goal 6	Re-engineer/use end-to-end business processes[a] to reduce transaction times, drive down costs, and improve service
Goal 7	Create agile business operations that plan for, support, and sustain contingency missions

Source: DOD.

[a]According to DOD, end-to-end business processes are business processes that span core business areas, cutting across functional areas and organizations. There are 15 end-to-end business processes, such as Hire-to-Retire and Procure-to-Pay.

Each of these goals has associated initiatives for achieving specific outcomes as well as measures for assessing progress. In addition, for each goal, DOD identified goal owners—senior leaders with responsibilities for ensuring success and reporting quarterly progress on SMP goals. The goal owners are the Under Secretary of Defense (Personnel and Readiness); Under Secretary of Defense (Acquisition, Technology, and Logistics); the Comptroller; DOD Chief Information Officer, and the DOD Deputy Chief Management Officer. See appendix II for a more-detailed overview of DOD's fiscal year 2012-2013 SMP. DOD officials stated that they used a collaborative process to develop the fiscal year 2012-2013 SMP. According to DOD officials, the DCMO solicited input from across the department, including the offices of the Under Secretary of Defense for Personnel and Readiness; the Under Secretary of Defense for Acquisition, Technology and Logistics; the Comptroller; the DOD Chief Information Officer; and the military departments. The Under Secretaries identified the goals, initiatives, and measures to be included in the SMP. Military department officials stated that they provided input on the SMP goals and believe that these goals are consistent with the military departments' business priorities.

Our analysis shows that the fiscal year 2012-2013 SMP now includes some key strategic planning elements that were lacking from previous plans. Specifically, as discussed below, we note that the fiscal year 2012-2013 SMP aligns business goals to department-wide goals, links its business goals to other business-related plans, and contains improved performance measures.

SMP Goals Align to Department-wide Goals

The 2009 SMP did not clearly link its business goals with department-wide goals because, at the time, the department was midway through its development of the 2010 Quadrennial Defense Review (QDR). However, the fiscal year 2012-2013 SMP now states how each business goal is linked to high-level departmental goals in the 2010 QDR. For example, the SMP links DOD's business goal 1, "Strengthen the DOD Total Workforce Mix" with three of the QDR's strategic goals: strategic goal 1, "Prevail in Today's Wars"; strategic goal 3, "Prepare to Defeat Adversaries and Succeed in a Wide Range of Contingencies"; and strategic goal 4, "Preserve and Enhance the All-Volunteer Force." These efforts are consistent with our prior work stating that performance goals should align with an agency's long-term strategic goals and department-wide priorities in order to provide managers and staff with a road map showing how their work contributes to achieving strategic goals.[14]

SMP Identifies Other Business-Related Plans

In addition to the SMP, DOD has other strategic plans that support individual business areas. Linking SMP business goals to other strategic plans provides a more complete picture of DOD's efforts in its various business areas. Although previous SMPs noted that DOD utilizes a family of plans to guide its business-related efforts and generally described the existence of such other departmental plans, they did not specifically identify these plans or link them to SMP business goals. The fiscal year 2012-2013 SMP now identifies some plans and explicitly links them to some of the goals. For example, the description of the SMP business goal on DOD's information technology management mentions DOD's Information Technology Enterprise Strategy and Roadmap as the guide for achieving the initiatives associated with this business goal. Similarly, the narrative describing a business goal on increasing DOD's operational and installation energy efficiency states that DOD's recently published Operational Energy Strategy provides guidance for achieving operational energy efficiencies in support of this overarching SMP goal. As another example, the fiscal year 2012-2013 SMP goal on strengthening DOD financial management identifies the Financial Improvement and Audit Readiness Plan as providing the strategy and methodology to integrate, among other things, the department and components' financial plans.

SMP Contains Performance Measures with Milestones and Target Data

The fiscal year 2012-2013 SMP also includes some improvements to performance measures, specifically to include milestone or target data that would enable DOD to assess progress in achieving SMP goals. In our prior work, we found that 20 of the 76 performance measures in the 2009 SMP, or 26 percent, contained target data. The fiscal year 2012-2013 SMP improves upon this by providing milestones and target data for 58 of its 62 performance measures, or 94 percent. For example, the 2009 SMP calls for DOD to generally monitor the percent of Major Automated Information Systems that experienced cost and schedule increases per fiscal year. However, the fiscal year 2012-2013 SMP provides two measures that establish specific numerical targets by fiscal year for the number of "significant" and "critical" breaches for Major Automated

---

[14]GAO, *Defense Management: Tools for Measuring and Managing Defense Agency Performance Could Be Strengthened*, GAO-04-919 (Washington, D.C.: Sept. 13, 2004).

Information Systems.[15] Such milestone or target data is useful because it facilitates future assessments of whether overall goals and objectives are being achieved.

DOD's SMP Continues to Lack Some Key Information Needed to Provide Strategic Direction For Department-wide Business Transformation Efforts

While DOD has made some improvements to the fiscal year 2012-2013 SMP, it still lacks some key information, including (1) a description of key challenges and underlying root causes of systemic weaknesses the plan is intended to address; (2) sufficient context explaining why business goals and strategies in the current plan were chosen, and why those from prior SMPs were not included; (3) performance measures that fully reflect core activities needed to assess progress; and (4) funding priorities linked to goals. Until DOD takes steps to address these issues, it may not be fully focused on addressing the underlying causes that are contributing to its business challenges.

SMP Does Not Describe Scope of Business Transformation Challenges for Some Goals and Initiatives

The fiscal year 2012-2013 SMP does not fully describe the specific challenges that DOD's business goals are intended to address and what the root causes of those challenges are. Such information would establish a clear and common understanding of the systemic weaknesses the SMP is trying to address, and could allow the SMP to serve as a basis for establishing priorities to reform business operations and address any gaps. We found that the seven business goals in the SMP varied in the extent to which they described the scope of challenges and root causes of systemic weaknesses being addressed. For example:

- According to the fiscal year 2012-2013 SMP, the business goal on strengthening DOD's acquisition processes is aimed at obtaining greater efficiency and productivity in defense spending, but the SMP narrative accompanying this goal does not provide any information on what is causing the cost growth for DOD's major defense acquisition programs or on how the goal's initiatives may address those causes. Our work has shown that many factors contribute to cost growth,

---

[15]According to the fiscal year 2012-2013 SMP, a significant breach is defined as equal to or greater than 15 percent of the Acquisition Program Baseline total cost or with schedule slippages greater than 6 months. A critical breach is defined as equal to or greater than 25 percent of the Acquisition Program Baseline total cost or with schedule slippages greater than 1 year.

including the lack of well-defined requirements and sufficient information on technology at key points in the acquisition process.[16]

- In addition, the fiscal year 2012-2013 SMP narrative for the business goal on building agile and secure information technology capabilities states that the department must provide a synchronized and responsive capability for the DOD information enterprise, but does not describe the challenges to be addressed. Our work has shown that such challenges include that the department lacks a reliable, comprehensive inventory of all defense business systems, and has not fully defined and established a family of business system modernization management controls that is vital to ensuring that its business system investments are the right solutions for addressing its business needs and that its business system investments are managed to produce expected capabilities efficiently and cost-effectively.[17]

- The fiscal year 2012-2013 SMP also includes a business goal to reengineer and use business processes to reduce transaction times, drive down costs, and improve services. Associated with this goal is an initiative to "improve the supply chain end-to-end process" as well as measures that relate to the percentage of filling orders and customer wait time. However, the narrative describing the goal does not discuss the supply chain, including what aspects of the process need improvement. Our work has shown that deficiencies exist in several areas of the supply chain, such as materiel distribution, requirements forecasting, and asset visibility.[18]

---

[16]GAO, *Defense Management: Guidance and Progress Measures Are Needed to Realize Benefits from Changes in DOD's Joint Requirements Process*, GAO-12-339 (Washington, D.C.: Feb. 24, 2012); and *Defense Acquisitions: Strong Leadership Is Key to Planning and Executing Stable Weapons Programs*, GAO-10-522 (Washington, D.C.: May 6, 2010).

[17]GAO, *DOD Business Systems Modernization: Governance Mechanisms for Implementing Management Controls Need to Be Improved*, GAO-12-685 (Washington, D.C.: June 1, 2012); and GAO-11-278.

[18]GAO, *Defense Logistics: DOD Has Taken Actions to Improve Some Segments of the Materiel Distribution System*, GAO-12-883R (Washington, D.C.: Aug. 3, 2012); *Defense Logistics: Improvements Needed to Enhance DOD's Management Approach and Implementation of Item Unique Identification Technology*, GAO-12-482 (Washington, D.C.: May 3, 2012); and *Defense Inventory: Defense Logistics Agency Needs to Expand on Efforts to More Effectively Manage Spare Parts*, GAO-10-469 (Washington, D.C.: May 11, 2010).

- The plan includes a business goal to create agile business operations that plan for, support, and sustain contingency missions. This goal includes an initiative to "institutionalize operational contract support." However, the plan does not explain the challenges DOD is encountering in the area of operational contract support and what aspects of this area need to be addressed. Our work has shown that such challenges include insufficient capacity to oversee contractors and inadequate planning for contractor support during contingency operations.[19] Further, the plan does not address the challenges confronted by DOD in other contract management–related areas, including how DOD acquires services, ensuring the appropriate use of contracting approaches, and enhancing the capacity of the acquisition workforce.

With additional information on the scope and root causes of challenges, DOD would more effectively communicate business priorities and focus initiatives to ensure that the department is addressing long-term systemic challenges in business areas. Moreover, without a description of key business challenges, the department cannot be assured that it has identified the appropriate initiatives and performance measures to assess progress in addressing those challenges.

SMP Does Not Always Provide Sufficient Context for Business Goals

The fiscal year 2012-2013 SMP does not include sufficient context explaining the basis for selecting the seven overarching business goals, such as why these goals were considered high priorities for DOD. According to guidance from the Office of Management and Budget (OMB) on developing agency strategic plans, plans should provide sufficient context to explain the basis for why specific goals and strategies are

---

[19]GAO, *Iraq and Afghanistan: DOD, State, and USAID Face Continued Challenges in Tracking Contracts, Assistance Instruments, and Associated Personnel,* GAO-11-1 (Washington, D.C.: Oct. 1, 2010); *Warfighter Support: Cultural Change Needed to Improve How DOD Plans for and Manages Operational Contract Support,* GAO-10-829T (Washington, D.C.: June 29, 2010); and *Warfighter Support: DOD Needs to Improve Its Planning for Using Contractors to Support Future Military Operations,* GAO-10-472 (Washington, D.C.: Mar. 30, 2010).

chosen.[20] However, some business goals and strategies have changed with each SMP without any context for why these changes have occurred, such as whether sufficient progress has been made to warrant the changes. For example, prior SMPs included goals that addressed the business area of support infrastructure management, which includes the maintenance, support, and disposal of installation facilities. DOD's infrastructure is critical to maintaining military readiness, with the cost to build and maintain this infrastructure representing a significant financial commitment. The 2009 SMP contained an objective on improving real property installation management under the financial management goal. The 2011 SMP contained the same objective, but placed it under its goal on reforming the DOD acquisition and support processes. However, the fiscal year 2012-2013 SMP no longer lists a goal or objective related to support infrastructure and does not explain why the area has been removed, such as any assessment done on progress in the area to justify its removal. Support infrastructure management has been on GAO's high-risk list since 1997. Moreover, we have recently reported that DOD continues to face significant challenges in this area, specifically in reducing excess facilities and in achieving efficiencies and cost savings in implementing joint bases and common support base standards.[21] Without sufficient context on why this area has been removed despite ongoing challenges, it is unclear whether DOD believes that support infrastructure—related objectives in the prior SMPs were achieved, or whether its priorities have changed. Moreover, without clear criteria for removing or changing key goals, particularly those related to high-risk areas, it may be difficult for DOD to demonstrate tangible results.

---

[20]Office of Management and Budget, *Performance Improvement Guidance: Management Responsibilities and Government Performance and Results Act Documents,* Memorandum M-10-24 (June 25, 2010). According to this memorandum, providing sufficient context is an important strategic planning element that should be included in Government Performance and Results Act (GPRA) documents to make them more useful to agency leadership, managers, and employees. While GPRA does not directly apply to the SMP, our prior work has identified many of GPRA's requirements as the foundation for effective strategic planning.

[21]GAO, *Excess Facilities: DOD Needs More Complete Information and a Strategy to Guide Its Future Disposal Efforts,* GAO-11-814 (Washington, D.C.: May 3, 2012); and *DOD Joint Bases: Management Improvements Needed to Achieve Greater Efficiencies,* GAO-13-134 (Washington, D.C.: Nov. 15, 2012).

Similarly, the fiscal year 2012-2013 SMP does not discuss the military departments' business priorities and how they link to the SMP's business goals. Previous SMPs included information on each of the military departments' top priorities, which, they stated, were aimed at achieving integrated management of business operations. The military departments play a key role in DOD's efforts to transform its business operations, representing a significant portion of DOD's organization and resources. The Under Secretary of each military department serves as its CMO with primary responsibility for business operations and for developing and executing a business transformation plan for that military department. The Army and Navy have business transformation plans, and Air Force officials stated that they have a draft business transformation plan. Given these responsibilities, it is important that DOD's plan outline the expected contribution of the military departments and the accountability of their CMOs in achieving department-wide business goals. However, the fiscal year 2012-2013 SMP does not discuss the military departments' business-related priorities or explain why this information is no longer included. In the absence of such information, DOD decision makers lack context to fully understand how the military departments' business-related activities contribute to department-wide business transformation efforts.

SMP Performance Measures Do Not Fully Reflect Core Activities Needed to Assess Progress

The fiscal year 2012-2013 SMP includes performance measures that, in many cases, do not fully reflect core activities that are needed to address longstanding challenges and assess progress against DOD's business goals. While the SMP does not need to include all possible business transformation measures, our prior work has shown that performance measures should focus on core activities that would help managers assess whether they are achieving organizational goals.[22] However, we identified several examples where DOD's measures do not address some key challenges.

- The fiscal year 2012-2013 SMP includes one initiative on improving the supply chain end-to-end process. The performance measures associated with this initiative focus on customer wait time and delivery of the right part to the customer on time, in the correct quantity, and with no material deficiencies (typically referred to as perfect order fulfillment). While these are important performance measures, other issues that we have identified as focus areas for improvement in

---

[22]GAO, *Tax Administration: IRS Needs to Further Refine Its Tax Filing Season Performance Measures*, GAO-03-143, (Washington, D.C.: Nov. 22, 2002).

GAO's supply chain management high-risk area, such as asset visibility and requirements forecasting, are not fully addressed by these performance measures. We have previously reported that, although performance measures monitoring customer wait time and perfect order fulfillment allow DOD to track many aspects of supply chain performance, these measures do not allow DOD to assess the overall effectiveness and efficiency of the supply chain across the enterprise.[23] Additionally, we have reported that these measures are limited in their ability to guide the department's improvement efforts for supply chain management, specifically the focus areas for improvement—requirements forecasting, materiel distribution, and asset visibility—in GAO's supply chain high-risk area.[24] Customer wait time, for example, could fail to accurately measure the impact of supply chain management improvement initiatives, as this measure is influenced by many external factors. Further, our work demonstrates that DOD continues to face other problems in supply chain management.[25] For example, in the area of asset visibility, DOD has incomplete data on the number of items in its inventory that qualify for marking with Item Unique Identification technology[26] labels and lacks assurance that contractors are sufficiently marking newly-acquired items.[27] We have also reported on a number of challenges regarding DOD's ability to accurately forecast inventory needs.[28] Although DOD has a separate inventory management improvement plan, none of the measures for this area are included in the SMP.

---

[23]GAO, *Defense Logistics: DOD Needs to Take Additional Actions to Address Challenges in Supply Chain Management*, GAO-11-569 (Washington, D.C.: July 28, 2011).

[24]GAO, *DOD's High-Risk Areas: Progress Made Implementing Supply Chain Management Recommendations, but Full Extent of Improvement Unknown*, GAO-07-234 (Washington, D.C.: Jan. 17, 2007).

[25] GAO-12-883R; GAO-12-482; and *Defense Inventory: Actions Underway to Implement Improvement Plan, but Steps Needed to Enhance Efforts*, GAO-12-493 (Washington, D.C.: May 3, 2012).

[26]Item Unique Identification technology allows DOD to assign a unique number to an individual item and then use that unique number to manage that item in a variety of logistics processes.

[27]GAO-12-482.

[28]GAO, *Defense Inventory: Defense Logistics Agency Needs to Expand on Efforts to More Effectively Manage Spare Parts*, GAO-10-469 (Washington, D.C.: May 11, 2010).

- The fiscal year 2012-2013 SMP's performance measures for DOD's workforce-related goal also do not fully address core elements of DOD's workforce, such as civilian and contractor components of the total workforce. For example, the SMP contains a goal on strengthening and right-sizing the DOD total workforce mix, and a related initiative to recruit and retain the right quality skilled personnel to meet mission requirements. The plan includes measures related to DOD's progress in recruiting sufficient numbers of military personnel against prescribed end-strength goals and the percentage of military recruits that have high school diplomas and meet other criteria. However, the plan does not include additional measures to assess whether DOD is recruiting and retaining civilian staff with the right mix of skills and competencies, such as financial management and acquisition skills. Our past work has shown that this is an important challenge and that DOD has not yet fully completed statutorily mandated gap assessments of its skills and competencies needed to develop the right recruiting and retention goals.[29] Further, the fiscal year 2012-2013 SMP does not have measures for evaluating any aspect of the contractor workforce or any aspect of the civilian workforce beyond the Civilian Expeditionary Workforce.[30] Therefore, the plan does not have a balanced set of measures to help address whether DOD has the core activities needed to assess progress toward strengthening and right-sizing DOD military, civilian, and contractor personnel who constitute the total workforce.

- In the area of operational contract support, the fiscal year 2012-2013 SMP identifies some measures related to planning for contractor support, including the percent of geographic combatant command plans that have been reviewed and analyzed with regard to determining the nature of contractor support that may be needed in future contingencies, but does not address other challenges that affect DOD's contingency operations, including the lack of trained contract oversight personnel.[31]

---

[29] GAO, *Human Capital: DOD Needs Complete Assessments to Improve Future Civilian Strategic Workforce Plans*, GAO-12-1014 (Washington, D.C.: Sept. 27, 2012).

[30] DOD established the Civilian Expeditionary Workforce in January 2009 to serve as a source for deployable civilians.

[31] GAO-10-829T.

SMP Does Not Include Funding Priorities

We previously reported that DOD's 2009 SMP did not identify funding priorities or resources needed to achieve goals, and therefore, we recommended that the revised SMP contain funding priorities linked to goals.[32] However, the fiscal year 2012-2013 SMP does not discuss resource needs or funding priorities among the business goals and initiatives. Our prior work has shown that agencies are successful in achieving business management transformation when they strive to establish strategic plans that prioritize initiatives and resources. The SMP lists key initiatives for achieving each business goal, but it does not discuss resource needs or prioritize initiatives so that activities can be linked to funding decisions. Rather, the SMP contains a general statement that DOD reviews and approves plans and budgets for business operations through the department's established budget cycle. Without including a description of funding priorities or resource needs, DOD decision makers cannot be assured that they are developing plans and budget requests that reflect business priorities. Therefore, we continue to believe that our prior recommendation to include this information has merit.

Further refining the SMP to include key information—such as a description of the scope of key business challenges, sufficient context for its goals, improved performance measures, and funding priorities—would more effectively assist DOD decision makers in targeting reform efforts to address systemic business challenges and in making investment decisions that reflect business priorities. DOD officials acknowledged that the SMP lacks some key information, but stated that the SMP is still maturing and that they will address these limitations in future refinements of the SMP. For example, the military department CMOs agreed that the next SMP should clarify the linkage between the business priorities of the military departments and DOD as a whole. Also, with regard to performance measures, officials from the office of the DCMO stated that, in developing the SMP, they recognized that the performance measures did not represent the complete scope of measures needed to assess progress against business goals. Officials from the office of the DCMO stated they will rely on continuous collaboration with the Under Secretaries of Defense and the military departments to further refine performance measures that more fully address business goal challenges and include these refined measures in future SMPs.

---

[32]GAO-11-181R.

DOD is Limited in Its Ability to Assess Department-wide Progress Toward Achieving Business Transformation Goals

DOD has broadly outlined a performance management approach for business transformation and begun to collect performance information, but has not fully demonstrated how its governance structures will use available performance information from various sources to assess department-wide progress against business goals.

DOD Has Broadly Outlined a Performance Management Approach

DOD has assigned performance responsibilities and broadly outlined its performance management approach, including steps for setting performance targets, reporting and assessing performance data, and taking corrective action. Under GPRA, the Deputy Secretary of Defense, as CMO, is responsible for improving the management and performance of the agency.[33] GPRA also gives the DCMO responsibility for advising and assisting the CMO in areas like goal-setting, planning, and performance measurement.[34] In addition, the 2009 SMP generally describes the performance management roles and responsibilities of the CMO and DCMO. The CMO is to define performance goals for business operations and review progress periodically against those goals, and the DCMO is to advise the CMO on performance goals and measures, and to assess progress.

DOD has also identified key steps and various governance structures that are a part of its performance management approach to advance business initiatives throughout the department. The 2009 SMP outlined six steps reflecting key decision points within DOD's performance management approach: planning; setting targets; cascading measures so that they align to a common set of priorities; aligning processes; assessing and

---

[33]31 U.S.C. §1123. GPRA states that, at each agency, the deputy head of agency, or equivalent, shall be the chief operating officer of the agency. The CMO serves as the chief operating officer of DOD for purposes of GPRA.

[34]31 U.S.C. §1124. GPRA states that, at each agency, the head of the agency, in consultation with the agency chief operating officer, shall designate a senior executive of the agency as the agency performance improvement officer. The DCMO serves as the agency performance improvement officer for purposes of GPRA. For general information on the roles and responsibilities of the CMO and DCMO, see DOD Directive 5105.02, *Deputy Secretary of Defense* (Oct. 18, 2011) and DOD Directive 5105.82, *Deputy Chief Management Officer (DCMO) of the Department of Defense* (Oct. 17, 2008).

reporting results; and taking corrective action. In this plan, DOD listed the governance structures that are, among other things, responsible for assessing and monitoring progress being made toward achieving the department's business goals. For example, the plan identified the Defense Business Systems Management Committee as a key senior-level board for assisting the CMO in his performance management responsibilities.[35] The fiscal year 2012-2013 SMP further outlined this performance management approach by identifying governance structures associated with each goal that, combined with the Defense Business Systems Management Committee, will form the mechanism through which DOD leaders review business priorities. For example, the plan states that DOD will use governance structures, such as the Senior Readiness Oversight Council, to help oversee and monitor progress toward achieving the goal on strengthening the DOD workforce.

Following the issuance of the fiscal year 2012-2013 SMP, DOD established two governance structures that are intended, in part, to monitor business transformation progress. Specifically, in October 2011, the Deputy Secretary of Defense established the Deputy's Management Action Group (DMAG);[36] a senior-level forum that meets several times a month to discuss various department-wide management issues. According to the memorandum establishing the DMAG, the Deputy Secretary of Defense will use the DMAG to develop a common management approach to disparate topics and processes to ensure that management actions are synchronized and fully coordinated across the defense enterprise. In addition, DOD established the Defense Business Council (DBC), which is chaired by the DCMO and began meeting in

---

[35]DOD established the Defense Business Systems Management Committee under the authority of section 332 of the Ronald W. Reagan National Defense Authorization Act for Fiscal Year 2005 and 10 U.S.C. §186, which required the department to set up a committee to review and approve major updates of the defense business enterprise architecture and to ensure that the obligation of funds for defense systems modernization is consistent with the criteria set out in 10 U.S.C. § 2222.

[36]Deputy Secretary of Defense Memorandum, *Management Process for the Deputy Secretary of Defense* (Oct. 6, 2011).

June 2012.[37] According to the DBC's charter, which was issued in October 2012, the DBC will recommend certification of business systems investments and is also responsible, among other things, for improving the department's business activities and management structures.[38] In addition, officials from the Office of the DCMO stated that the DBC, rather than the Defense Business Systems Management Committee, will now serve as the primary forum for reviewing SMP quarterly performance results and discussing business-related performance topics.

DOD Is Collecting and Reporting Business-Related Performance Information and Undertaking Various Business-Related Reform Activities

The Office of the DCMO has a process in place whereby goal owners responsible for implementing SMP goals report progress on SMP measures on a quarterly basis. For example, the Under Secretary of Defense for Personnel and Readiness is responsible for ensuring the success of the SMP goal related to strengthening the DOD total workforce mix. In order to assess progress toward this goal, the Under Secretary of Defense for Personnel and Readiness reports quarterly to the Office of the DCMO on the status of the 10 measures associated with the goal.

In addition to collecting SMP performance information, DOD has set up procedures and assigned responsibility for collecting and reporting business –related performance information related to other plans for specific business areas, the department's annual performance plan, agency priority goals, and numerous business reform activities as described below.

---

[37]The DBC members are: Deputy Chief Management Officer; Assistant Secretary of Defense (Acquisition); Assistant Secretary of Defense (Logistics & Materiel Readiness); Deputy Under Secretary of Defense (Installations & Environment); Director, Defense Procurement and Acquisition Policy; Deputy Chief Financial Officer; Deputy Comptroller (Programs/Budgets); Director, Personnel and Readiness Information Management, Office of the Under Secretary of Defense (Personnel & Readiness); Director of Intelligence, Surveillance, and Reconnaissance Programs, Office of the Under Secretary of Defense (Intelligence); Chief Operating Officer, Office of the Under Secretary of Defense (Policy); Office of Joint Chiefs of Staff (J6); Deputy DOD Chief Information Officer; the Department of the Army DCMO; Department of the Navy DCMO; Department of the Air Force DCMO; Comptroller and Director of Administration and Management (National Guard Bureau); Deputy Director, Program Evaluation (Cost Assessment and Program Evaluation); Office of the General Counsel; and the Director, Office of Business Transformation (Army).

[38] Deputy Chief Management Officer Memorandum, *Defense Business Council* (Oct. 18, 2012).

- DOD collects and reports performance information on other business-related plans, which may contain additional measures beyond those included in the SMP. For example, the Under Secretaries of Defense for Acquisition, Technology, and Logistics and the Comptroller respectively collect performance data on measures from separate business-related plans, such as the Logistics Strategic Plan and the Financial Improvement and Audit Readiness Plan. Similarly, the military departments collect information on the business priorities outlined in their respective business transformation or departmental plans.

- DOD also collects and reports business-related performance information as part of its annual performance plan—a plan called for by GPRA,[39] which requires federal agencies to, among other things, prepare annual performance plans that establish objective, quantifiable, and measurable goals for the upcoming fiscal year; describe how those goals contribute to the agency's long-term strategic goals; as well as provide the indicators the agency will use to measure performance against the goals. The Office of the Secretary of Defense Principal Staff Assistants,[40] which include the Under Secretaries of Defense, collect and report quarterly on progress on measures for the department's five strategic goals, one of which focuses on reforming DOD's business and support functions.

- The Under Secretaries of Defense also report quarterly on progress toward achieving DOD's five agency priority goals. GPRA, as amended, requires the heads of certain executive agencies to identify a subset of the performance goals from their agency performance plan as "agency priority goals."[41] These goals are intended to reflect the highest priorities of the agency. In addition, the "agency priority goals" are required to have ambitious targets that can be achieved within a 2-year period and are to have clearly defined quarterly

[39]31 U.S.C. §1115.

[40]The Office of the Secretary of Defense Principal Staff Assistants are the Under Secretaries of Defense; the Assistant Secretaries of Defense; the Director, Operational Test and Evaluation; the General Counsel of the Department of Defense; the Inspector General of the Department of Defense; and the Office of the Secretary of Defense Directors or equivalents who report directly to the Secretary of Defense or the Deputy Secretary of Defense.

[41]31 U.S.C. §1120.

GAO-13-267 Defense Business Transformation

milestones. According to DOD, these goals are intended to reflect priorities or near-term improvements that advance progress toward the longer-term outcomes identified in DOD's performance plan. For example, DOD has a priority goal on audit readiness that sets a specific near-term milestone for improving the accuracy and reliability of the department's recorded appropriated funds, which supports DOD's broader performance plan goal of reforming the business and support functions of the department.

In addition, at any given time, DOD is undertaking and monitoring implementation of various reform activities across the department in order to improve business operations. For example, the Under Secretary of Defense for Acquisition, Technology and Logistics has multiple efforts underway to improve the department's acquisition processes known as the Better Buying Power initiative. Similarly, the military departments have specific initiatives aimed at improving acquisition processes, enhancing financial auditability, and consolidating information technology investments. Further, the Office of the DCMO has taken steps to standardize approaches, such as establishing a new process for overseeing defense business system investments, collaborating with the Deputy Chief Financial Officer to develop guidance on improved financial information, and working with some combatant commands to improve visibility of contract information.

DOD Has Not Fully Demonstrated How its Governance Structures Will Routinely Integrate Performance Information to Assess Department-wide Progress against Business Goals and Achieve Measurable Results

According to its charter, the DBC is responsible for, among other things, overseeing DOD's performance management programs.[42] More specifically, the charter states that the DBC is to review DOD's performance results to track progress against strategic goals and hold department leaders accountable for results. The DBC can also raise business and performance management issues to the DMAG as necessary. Our prior work has shown that management can promote the use of performance information by leading frequent, regular performance-review meetings to discuss progress made toward achievement of results, which can assist in identifying performance problems and in developing corrective actions.[43] According to DOD officials, the DBC will serve as the primary forum for discussing business related performance topics and for reviewing SMP quarterly results, and as necessary will raise issues to the DMAG for higher level review and action.

As discussed above, DOD collects performance information on SMP measures as well as from a variety of other sources. However, DOD has not used its governance structures to regularly review performance information or demonstrated how these structures will routinely integrate various sources of performance information to assess department-wide progress towards business goals. For example, DOD has assigned responsibility to the DBC to review performance results and track progress. As of December 2012, the Office of the DCMO has provided performance information to the DBC on two occasions. This information was focused on results related to the SMP and the annual performance plan. Specifically, in October 2012, the DBC reviewed summary information on third quarter of fiscal year 2012 performance results related to the SMP and DOD's annual performance plan. With regard to the SMP, the summary information consisted of a slide that indicated that, of the 61 performance measures in the fiscal year 2012-2013 SMP, 31 were on track, 11 were at risk of not meeting their targets, and 19 measures were either unavailable or only reported annually. In addition, the slide named the SMP measures at risk of not meeting quarterly targets or not being reported by goal owners. This information did not include a discussion of why the SMP measures were at risk or

---

[42]Deputy Chief Management Officer Memorandum, *Defense Business Council.*

[43]GAO, *Results-Oriented Management: Strengthening Key Practices at FEMA and Interior Could Promote Greater Use of Performance Information,* GAO-09-676 (Washington, D.C.: Aug. 17, 2009).

unavailable. Similarly, with regard to the department's annual performance plan, the DBC was provided with a slide that indicated that, of the 23 performance measures in the fiscal year 2012 annual performance plan related to the plan's goal to reform business and support functions, 14 were on track and 9 were at risk of not meeting their targets. Prior to the establishment of the DBC, DOD relied on the Defense Business Systems Management Committee to review SMP performance information. The Defense Business Systems Management Committee reviewed SMP quarterly performance three times in fiscal year 2010 and twice in fiscal year 2011.

The performance information provided to the DBC provides a partial picture of the department's performance in various business areas, limiting the ability of DOD to assess overall progress towards business goals. For example:

- Operational contract support: The fiscal year 2012-2013 SMP includes two measures related to its initiative on institutionalizing operational contract support. The third quarter fiscal year 2012 performance results briefed to the DBC indicate that these measures are on track to meet their targets. However, the measures provide a partial picture of the department's ongoing efforts to improve this business area. According to an official from the Office of the Under Secretary of Defense for Acquisition, Logistics, and Technology responsible for this initiative, the two measures reflect an important aspect of DOD's work in the area of operational contract support, but there are other issues that DOD needs to address in this area that the measures do not cover. For example, one of the measures pertains to the extent to which a particular database captures contract information; however, according to the official, this database captures only a subset of DOD's contractors, and DOD is currently using an additional system that is not mentioned in the SMP. Further, this official stated that there are a number of other efforts underway to improve operational contract support and that the measures in the SMP were intended to be a starting point for tracking progress in this business area. As a result, although the performance results briefed to the DBC indicate that the operational contract support initiative is on track, they do not address the department's progress or potential challenges regarding other ongoing efforts that affect operational contract support.

- Operational and installation energy efficiency: The fiscal year 2012-2013 SMP includes seven measures related to its goal on increasing operational and installation energy efficiency. In the third quarter fiscal year 2012 performance results briefed to the DBC, two of these measures were reported as being at risk of not meeting quarterly targets. According to officials from the Office of the Under Secretary of Defense for Acquisition, Logistics, and Technology —the goal owner responsible for operational and installation energy efficiency —these two measures only reflect a subset of the department's overall efforts to improve operational energy efficiency. For example, according to the officials, there is an Operational Energy Strategy and an Operational Energy Implementation Plan that lay out the department's approach to utilizing energy resources; however, the fiscal year 2012-2013 SMP measures only cover a portion of what is outlined in the Operational Energy Strategy. Specifically, the fiscal year 2012-2013 SMP addresses reducing operational energy consumption, but does not address issues related to operational energy supply and operational energy security, which are included in the Operational Energy Strategy. As a result, the performance results briefed to the DBC do not provide sufficient information to assess the department's progress on ongoing efforts that affect operational energy efficiency.

- Supply chain management: Both the fiscal year 2012-2013 SMP and the department's annual performance plan include four measures related to improving the supply chain process. The third-quarter fiscal year 2012 performance results briefed to the DBC indicated that these four measures were on track to meet their targets. In addition, the department's annual performance plan contains two measures related to inventory management, but, according to fourth-quarter fiscal year 2012 performance results on the annual performance plan, no information is available on these two measures until March 2013. However, as discussed earlier, these measures do not fully address the focus areas for improvement in GAO's supply chain high-risk area, such as some aspects of asset visibility and requirements forecasting, and our work demonstrates that DOD continues to face problems in supply chain management. DOD has a number of efforts underway to improve supply chain management, including efforts undertaken under separate business-related plans such as the Logistics Strategic Plan. Information on the department's progress under these efforts may not be fully reflected in the measures provided to the DBC, potentially limiting the department's understanding of other challenges in supply chain management.

Without integrating performance information from a broader range of sources to provide a more comprehensive picture of the department's performance across key business areas and regularly reviewing this integrated information, DOD cannot be assured that it is well-positioned to assess the overall impact of its efforts to achieve business transformation.

Conclusions

DOD business operations, such as management of finances, the supply chain, support infrastructure, and weapon systems acquisition provide essential support to the warfighter. Longstanding management weaknesses related to these business operations adversely affect DOD's efficiency and effectiveness and hinder its ability to free up resources for higher-priority needs. DOD has clearly taken steps to improve its management approach to business transformation, including further refining its SMP and collecting and reporting business-related performance information. However, additional information is needed in the plan to set strategic direction and therefore make it a more useful tool for decisionmakers as they target and implement reform initiatives. Furthermore, developing a performance management approach that enables DOD to integrate and assess business-related performance information in a holistic manner will further enhance DOD's ability to strategically focus the department's transformation efforts on the highest priority areas, assess department-wide progress against business goals, take corrective action to stay on course, and ultimately demonstrate tangible improvements in key business areas, including those that we have designated as high risk.

Recommendations for Executive Action

To enhance DOD's ability to set strategic direction for its business transformation efforts, better assess overall progress toward business transformation goals, and take any necessary corrective actions, we recommend that the Secretary of Defense direct the Deputy Secretary of Defense, in his capacity as the Chief Management Officer (CMO), to take the following actions:

- Ensure that the SMP includes a description of the key business transformation challenges to be addressed, sufficient context for why specific goals and strategies were chosen, and measures to address core activities.

- Further define DOD's performance management approach, by outlining elements such as how it will consider the various sources of performance information along with SMP performance results to monitor progress in achieving business goals and identify corrective actions and ensure this information is reviewed on a regular basis.

Agency Comments and Our Evaluation

In written comments on a draft of this report, DOD partially concurred with our first recommendation and concurred with our second recommendation. The full text of DOD's written comments is reprinted in appendix III.

In its overall comments, DOD stated the department appreciates our recognition of the significant progress that has been made since first designating the DOD Approach to Business Transformation as a high-risk area in 2005. DOD noted that, at that time, we stated we made the designation because "DOD had not established management responsibility, accountability, and control over business transformation-related activities and resources, and it lacked a plan for business transformation with specific goals, measures, and mechanisms to monitor progress." DOD added that, while the department recognizes that more work is needed to fully mature the SMP and its performance management system, it believes that it has fully remediated each of these original root causes. We will be providing our assessment of the department's progress in strengthening its approach to business transformation in the upcoming update to our high-risk series.

DOD partially concurred with our first recommendation that the Secretary of Defense direct the Deputy Secretary of Defense to ensure that the SMP includes a description of the key business transformation challenges to be addressed, sufficient context for why specific goals and strategies were chosen, and measures to address core activities. In its comments, DOD stated that future releases of the SMP will include this information. However, DOD expressed concern that we appear to advocate for an expansive vision of the SMP that misunderstands the broader management framework surrounding it, and made a number of observations about our report. DOD stated that the SMP, and the subsequent tracking of the department's performance against it, is not intended to capture every important business improvement activity. Rather, DOD stated, the SMP exists within the context of a broader family of plans that supports and aligns to the SMP's highest-level business goals. It also noted that, while performance measures can be improved, it is important to acknowledge that even an improved SMP will include only a small set of measures and that other important measures will continue to be managed through the department's established management framework.

We agree that the SMP is part of DOD's broader management approach. For example, our report recognizes that DOD utilizes a broader family of plans to guide its business transformation, and that the SMP showed improvement by linking to some of these plans. We also agree that the SMP will include a smaller set of measures than those used by various organizations throughout the department. For example, our report recognizes that DOD collects and reports progress against other business related plans, which may contain additional measures beyond those included in the SMP. While we agree the SMP does not need to include all possible measures, our prior work has shown that performance measures should focus on core activities that would help managers assess whether they are achieving organizational goals. However, we identified several examples where DOD's measures in the SMP do not address core activities in some key business areas, such as asset visibility and requirements forecasting for the supply chain management area, and the availability of trained contract oversight personnel for the operational contract support area. To focus attention on those activities that are needed to address longstanding challenges and help DOD assess progress against its goals, we continue to believe that measures included in the SMP should reflect the core activities of the department's business goals.

Further, DOD concurred with our second recommendation that the Secretary of Defense direct the Deputy Secretary of Defense to further define DOD's performance management approach by outlining elements such as how it will consider the various sources of performance information along with SMP performance results to monitor progress in achieving business goals and identify corrective actions, and ensure that this information is reviewed on a regular basis. In its comments, DOD stated that the department will continue to improve and institutionalize operations of the Defense Business Council to provide unified direction and leadership to efficiently and effectively manage the DOD business mission area. As part of these efforts, GAO believes that DOD needs to identify specific steps it will take to integrate and regularly review various sources of performance information along with the SMP performance results to monitor progress and identify corrective actions. Without integrating performance information from a broader range of sources to provide a more comprehensive picture of the department's performance across key business areas and regularly reviewing this integrated information, DOD cannot be assured that it is well-positioned to assess the overall impact of its business transformation efforts.

We are sending copies of this report to the appropriate congressional committees. We are also sending copies to the Secretary of Defense, the Deputy Secretary of Defense, the DOD Deputy Chief Management Officer (DCMO), and the Under Secretaries of the Army, Navy, and Air Force. In addition, the report will also be available on our website at http://www.gao.gov. If you or your staff have questions about this report, please contact me at (202)-512-9619 or pickups@gao.gov. Contact points for our Offices of Congressional Relations and Public Affairs may be found on the last page of this report. Key contributors to this report are listed in appendix IV.

Sharon L. Pickup
Director
Defense Capabilities and Management

List of Committees

The Honorable Carl Levin
Chairman
The Honorable James M. Inhofe
Ranking Member
Committee on Armed Services
United States Senate

The Honorable Tom Carper
Chairman
The Honorable Tom Coburn
Ranking Member
Committee on Homeland Security
   and Governmental Affairs
United States Senate

The Honorable Howard P. McKeon
Chairman
The Honorable Adam Smith
Ranking Member
Committee on Armed Services
House of Representatives

The Honorable Darrell E. Issa
Chairman
The Honorable Elijah Cummings
Ranking Member
Committee on Oversight
   and Government Reform
House of Representatives

Appendix I: Scope and Methodology

To assess what additional steps the Department of Defense (DOD) has taken to incorporate key strategic planning elements into its business transformation plan, we evaluated relevant documentation and interviewed knowledgeable officials. Specifically, we reviewed DOD's Fiscal Year 2012-2013 Strategic Management Plan, as well as DOD's previous Strategic Management Plans for 2008, 2009, and Fiscal Year 2011. We assessed whether the Fiscal Year 2012-2013 Strategic Management Plan included key elements that we have previously identified as needed for effective strategic planning, such as alignment with higher- and lower-level organizational plans, successful performance measures, inclusion of funding priorities, description of the scope of the problem, and inclusion of sufficient context. In assessing this plan, we also relied on prior and ongoing work we have conducted in individual DOD business areas, namely, DOD workforce management, financial management, business systems modernization, supply chain management, energy efficiency, support infrastructure management, weapon systems acquisition, and contract management. In addition, we reviewed other DOD documentation, such as the 2010 Quadrennial Defense Review; DOD's annual performance plans for fiscal years 2011, 2012, and 2013; DOD's annual reports on business transformation to Congress; and relevant DOD directives and memos. We also reviewed strategic planning documents and annual reports to Congress issued by the business transformation offices of the Army, Navy, and Air Force.

To assess the extent to which DOD has developed an approach for assessing department-wide progress toward business transformation goals, we reviewed relevant documents and interviewed senior DOD officials about the department's performance assessment approach and its related governance mechanisms for monitoring business transformation progress. Specifically, we reviewed DOD's Strategic Management Plans for 2009 and Fiscal Years 2012-2013; DOD's annual performance plans for fiscal years 2011, 2012, and 2013; DOD's quarterly performance results for these performance plans and for the Strategic Management Plan for fiscal years 2011 and 2012; DOD memos and directives; DOD guidance, meeting agendas, and briefing documents related to the Defense Business Systems Management Committee, the Defense Business Council, and the Deputy's Management Action Group; and other business-related strategic plans, such as the Logistics Strategic Plan and the Defense Installations Strategic Plan. We also evaluated the department's performance assessment approach in light of roles and responsibilities laid out in DOD's 2009 Strategic Management Plan and in the Government Performance and Results Act Modernization Act of 1993, as amended, and in light of key practices in results-oriented management, as identified in our previous work.

We visited or contacted the following organizations during our review:

- Office of the Deputy Secretary of Defense;

- Office of the Deputy Chief Management Officer;

- Office of the Under Secretary of Defense (Acquisition, Technology and Logistics);

- Office of the Under Secretary of Defense (Personnel and Readiness);

- Office of the Under Secretary of Defense (Comptroller) / Chief Financial Officer;

- Office of the Chief Information Officer;

- Offices of the Chief Management Officers and Deputy Chief Management Officers of the departments of the Army, Navy, and Air Force; and

- Business Transformation Offices within the departments of the Army, Navy, and Air Force.

We conducted this performance audit from February 2012 through February 2013 in accordance with generally accepted government auditing standards. Those standards require that we plan and perform the audit to obtain sufficient, appropriate evidence to provide a reasonable basis for our findings and conclusions based on our audit objectives. We believe that the evidence obtained provides a reasonable basis for our findings and conclusions based on our audit objectives.

Appendix II: Business Goals, Initiatives, and Measures in the Department of Defense's (DOD) Fiscal Year 2012-2013 Strategic Management Plan

Business Goal 1: Strengthen and right-size the Department of Defense (DOD) Total Workforce mix (military, civilian, and contracted support) to accomplish the DOD mission and sustain superior performance in a time of constrained resources

Initiatives	Measures[a]
• Recruit and retain the right-quality skilled personnel to meet mission requirements	• Percent variance (3% to 0%) in Active Component end-strength • Percent variance (3% to -3%) in Reserve Component end-strength • Percent of Tier 1 (High School Diploma Graduates) non-prior service Active Component accessions • Percent of Tier 1 (High School Diploma Graduates) non-prior service Reserve Component accessions • Percent of Category I-IIIA non-prior service Active Component accessions • Percent of Category I-IIIA non-prior service Reserve Component accessions • Percent of Category IV non-prior service Active Component accessions • Percent of Category IV non-prior service Reserve Component accessions
• Improve the readiness of the Civilian Expeditionary Workforce	• Percent of Emergency-Essential and Non-Combat Essential Civilian Expeditionary Workforce employees qualified as "ready", per the Civilian Expeditionary Workforce Readiness Index
• Increase the number of Special Forces personnel	• Cumulative percent increase in DOD Special Forces and Navy SEAL personnel achieved
• Develop and institutionalize a transparent, systemic, decision-making process to appropriately balance the DOD Total Workforce to ensure mission readiness	• Develop the initiative, milestones, and measures, and provide to the DOD Deputy Chief Management Officer not later than September 30, 2011

Business Goal 2: Strengthen DOD Financial Management to respond to warfighter needs and sustain public confidence through auditable financial statements

Initiatives	Measures
• Execute the Financial Improvement and Audit Readiness (FIAR) strategy and plans to achieve audit readiness by FY 2017	• Percent DOD Statement of Budgetary Resources Appropriations Received validated • Percent of DOD Funds Balance with Treasury validated • Percent of DOD Statement of Budgetary Resources validated • Percent of DOD mission-critical assets (Real Property, Military Equipment, General Equipment, Operating Materials and Supplies, and Inventory Balances) validated for existence and completeness
• By fiscal year 2012, once detailed supporting documentation is finalized, the DOD will ensure processing of Joint Urgent Operational Needs reprogrammings to meet a goal of approval within 2 congressional calendar months	• *None provided*
• By fiscal year 2012, DOD will achieve a commercial payment improper payment of 0.11 percent or less	• *None provided*

• By fiscal year 2013, the DOD will complete 16 interim milestones, which include validations of entities where Enterprise Resource Planning systems have been integrated, Major Defense Acquisition Programs, Fund Balance with Treasury Reconciliations, and Existence, and Completeness	• *None provided*

Business Goal 3: Build agile and secure information technology (IT) capabilities to enhance combat power and decision-making while optimizing value

Initiatives	Measures
• Execute the DOD IT Enterprise Strategy and Roadmap	• Reduce data centers by 18 percent in fourth quarter of fiscal year 2012 and an additional 12 percent in fourth quarter of fiscal year 2013 • Reduce networks by 10 percent in fourth quarter of fiscal year 212 and an additional 10 percent in fourth quarter of fiscal year 2013 • Percentage of services transitioned to, or designed as, Enterprise Services
• Strengthen the oversight of IT investments	• Percentage of component networks compliance with resilient network architecture and standards by all new investments and technology refresh activities by fourth quarter of fiscal year 2015
• Integrate cyber security across the DOD Information Enterprise	• Create and maintain strong boundary defenses across DOD NIPRNet Perimeter • NIPRNet Hardening allowing robust protection capabilities • Enforce Cryptographic Logon with PKI Hardware Tokens on SIPRNet • Reduce time to effect DOD network configuration changes
• Develop long-term strategy to provide for and protect mission critical access to radio frequency spectrum	• *None provided*

Business Goal 4: Increase the buying power of the DOD acquisition system and processes, spanning requirements determination, development, procurement, and support to ensure that the force structure is modernized, recapitalized, and sustained within available resources

Initiatives	Measures
• Implement and enforce affordability-based constraints on program acquisition and sustainment costs	• Mandate affordability as a requirement. Establish an affordability target as a Key Performance Parameter equivalent for all Acquisition Category I programs

• Improve acquisition processes to reduce costs and improve productivity for major defense acquisition programs, major automated information systems, and services	• Drive productivity by establishing "Should Cost" targets as management tools for all Acquisition Category I programs • Ensure service contracts that exceed $1 billion contain contract provisions to achieve productivity improvements and cost efficiencies throughout the contract term • Make production rates economical and hold them stable • Percent of enterprise level IT software and hardware national security and business systems deployed within 18 months of the capability business cases approval • Number of Major Automated Information System "significant" breaches (equal to or greater than 15% of Acquisition Program Baseline total cost or with schedule slippages greater than 6 months) • Number of Major Automated Information System "critical" breaches (equal to or greater than 25% of Acquisition Program Baseline total cost or with schedule slippages of one year or more)
• Increase the use of competition to control costs of goods and services	• Percentage of contract obligations that are competitively awarded • Competitive strategy to be provided as part of each Acquisition Category program's milestone acquisition strategy
• Improve the Department's rate of successful execution of buying plans reflected in the Future Years Defense Program	• Increase the percentage of Major Defense Acquisition Program items procured relative to the quantities requested over the previous year
• Increase the return on investment on science and technology spending	• Percent of completing demonstration programs transitioning each year
• Identify and preserve essential capabilities in the U.S. defense industrial base	• Complete first phase of Sector-by-Sector Tier-by-Tier effort • Identify and correct high visibility deficiencies in supplier base for critical weapon system components • Create a clearing house and repository of industrial base analyses for the Department and make it available to all services and organizations to reduce redundant efforts and establish best practices
• Provide incentives to industry to seek economies that drive down DOD procurement and life-cycle costs	• Include the incentive strategy behind the fee strategy in all acquisition strategies for all Acquisition Category 1D programs tying incentives to production and sustainment cost control • Increase the percentage of all efforts using Fixed Price Incentive Firm Target contracts that are moving from development to production and low-rate to full-rate production over the previous year's percentage
• Increase the productivity of each military department's acquisition system	• Demonstrate progress at reversing the trend to increasing unit costs in procured end items

Business Goal 5: Increase operational and installation energy efficiency to lower risks to our warfighters, reduce costs, and improve energy security

Initiatives	Measures
• Improve DOD's capability to measure and verify individual facility energy use	• Increase the number of facilities with installed meters
• Improve timeliness and accuracy of DOD's facility energy business decisions by exposing effective data to every authorized user in an automated and integrated manner	• Percent of enterprise energy systems fully utilizing the first module of the Enterprise Energy Information Management solution
• Reduce the risk from potential disruptions to the commercial grid to improve the energy security of installations	• Define and begin reporting standards for the following important energy security attributes:
	• (1) Contingency of operational planning (fiscal year 2012);
	• (2) Building design considerations (fiscal year 2012);
	• (3) Metering (fiscal year 2012);
	• (4) Smart grid systems and load management (fiscal year 2013);
	• (5) On-site generation (generators, renewables, etc.) (fiscal year 2013);
	• (6) Microgrid and system islanding (fiscal year 2013).
• Pursue DOD procurement or lease of plug-in electric vehicles for non-tactical fleet	• Numbers of leased/purchased plug-in electric vehicles and charging stations
• Expand the use of third party financing for energy projects	• Percentage of third party financed energy efficiency and renewable energy projects based on the DOD FY 2010 baseline
• Effectively manage Operational Energy use to reduce consumption	• Establish an operational energy baseline for DOD based on credible, verifiable point-of-use data
	• Establish and execute numerical energy reduction targets and timelines through rigorous data analysis and simulation efforts

Business Goal 6: Re-engineer/use end-to-end business processes to reduce transaction times, drive down costs, and improve service

Initiatives	Measures
• Improve the supply chain end-to-end process	• Perfect Order Fulfillment percentage for Defense Logistics Agency-stocked items
	• Army Customer Wait Time
	• Navy Customer Wait Time
	• Air Force Customer Wait Time
• Improve the cycle time to hire civilian employees	• Number of days for external civilian hiring (end-to-end timeline)
• Reduce support process transaction time at all levels	• *None provided*

GAO-13-267 Defense Business Transformation

• Improve business operations through optimal use of defense business systems and the Business Enterprise Architecture	• Percentage of Defense Business Systems/Services represented in both the DOD Information Technology Portfolio Repository and the Business Enterprise Architecture
	• Percentage of Defense Business Systems/Services represented in both the Select and Native Programming Data Input System – Information Technology and the Business Enterprise Architecture
	• Percentage of Defense Business Systems/Services reporting to the Office of Management and Budget through the Business Enterprise Architecture
• Complete mapping of end-to-end processes ("Hire-to-Retire" and "Procure-to-Pay" in fiscal year 2012-2013)	• Complete mapping of "Hire-to-Retire" and "Procure-to-Pay" end-to-end processes by end of fiscal year 2012; Determine processes outcome measure to monitor process improvement; Establish performance reporting processes
	• Determine next 2 end-to-end business processes to be completed by June 2013 and establish timelines for spirals of completion in fiscal year 2013
	• Complete mapping of both selected end-to-end business processes, determine processes outcome measures to monitor process improvement; establish performance reporting processes
	• Determine next 2 end-to-end business processes to be completed by end of fiscal year 2014 and establish timelines for spirals of completion in fiscal year 2014

Business Goal 7: Create agile business operations that plan for, support, and sustain contingency missions

Initiatives	Measures
• Institutionalize operational contract support	• Percent of geographic combatant command plans that have been reviewed/analyzed for Overseas Contingency Support Equities
	• Percent of contracts and contractor population properly registered in the Synchronized Pre-Deployment and Operational Tracker
• Establish complete visibility on contingency business operations to achieve accountability and build a comprehensive common operating picture	• Percentage of system traceability for all DOD funds obligated in theater, electronically capturing DOD approved and funded requirements, obligations, entitlements, and disbursements
• Adapt business processes to include operational criteria in order to execute the Commander of the NATO International Security Assistance Force/U.S. Forces-Afghanistan campaign plan	• Percentage of Afghan host nation vendors that are vetted and have with available past-performance information at contract close-out

Source: DOD.

[a]DOD's Fiscal Year 2012-2013 Strategic Management Plan also contains milestone data for many of the measures, but we did not include milestone data in this table.

Appendix III: Comments from the Department of Defense

Note: Page numbers in the draft report may differ from those in this report.

DEPUTY CHIEF MANAGEMENT OFFICER
9010 DEFENSE PENTAGON
WASHINGTON, DC 20301-9010

JAN

Ms. Sharon L. Pickup
Director, Defense Capabilities and Management
U.S. Government Accountability Office
441 G Street, NW
Washington, DC 20548

Dear Ms. Pickup,

This is the Department of Defense (DoD) response to the Government Accountability Office (GAO) draft report GAO-13-267, "DEFENSE BUSINESS TRANSFORMATION: Improvements Made but Additional Steps Needed to Strengthen Strategic Planning and Assess Progress," dated December 20, 2012, (GAO Code 351703). The Department partially concurs with the first recommendation and concurs with the second recommendation contained in the draft report.

The Department appreciates GAO's recognition of the significant progress that has been made since first designating the DoD Approach to Business Transformation as a high risk area in 2005. At that time, GAO stated that they made the designation because "DoD had not established management responsibility, accountability, and control over business transformation-related activities and resources, and it lacked a plan for business transformation with specific goals, measures, and mechanisms to monitor progress." While DoD recognizes that more work is needed to fully mature the Strategic Management Plan (SMP) and improve our performance management system, we believe that we have fully remediated each of these original root causes. Additionally, the Department remains concerned that GAO appears to advocate for an expansive vision of the SMP that misunderstands the broader management framework surrounding it and cannot be achieved.

The SMP, and the subsequent tracking of the Department's performance against it, is not intended to comprehensively capture each and every important business improvement activity taking place throughout the enterprise. Rather, the SMP exists within the context of a broader family of plans that supports and aligns to the SMP's highest level business goals. Through the crafting of SMP and in the execution of its performance management system, the Department's senior leaders make strategic choices about which broad goals are most important and, within those goals, on which initiatives and key indicators they will focus their management attention.

On the one hand, this report seems to acknowledge this point when it says, "While the SMP does not need to include all possible business transformation measures, our prior work has shown that performance measures should focus on core activities that would help managers assess whether they are achieving organizational goals." However, at the same time, the report contradicts this sentiment time and again when it critiques the SMP for not containing a measure reflecting every core element of every goal or not addressing every challenge in every business area.

The Department fully recognizes that it can improve in selecting the right performance measures to best assess whether we are achieving success, but it is important to acknowledge that even an improved SMP will include only a small set of measures – some worthy and important measures will not be included and will continued to be managed through the Department's established management framework. In the areas that GAO critiques the Department along these lines, such as infrastructure management, contract management, and operational energy, robust improvement efforts are underway and more comprehensive strategic plans are in place for the individual area. In these cases, the Department's efforts must be considered as an integrated whole, rather than by just looking at the SMP.

The Department appreciates the opportunity to comment on this draft report. Should you have any questions, please contact Mr. Thomas Cowley, 703-692-8170, thomas.cowley@osd.mil.

Sincerely,

Elizabeth A. McGrath

Enclosures:
As stated

2

GAO DRAFT REPORT DATED DECEMBER 20, 2012
GAO-13-267 (GAO CODE 351703)

"DEFENSE BUSINESS TRANSFORMATION: IMPROVEMENTS MADE BUT
ADDITIONAL STEPS NEEDED TO STRENGTHEN STRATEGIC PLANNING
AND ASSESS PROGRESS"

DEPARTMENT OF DEFENSE COMMENTS
TO THE GAO RECOMMENDATIONS

RECOMMENDATION 1: The GAO recommends that the Secretary of Defense direct
the Deputy Secretary of Defense, in his capacity as the Chief Management Officer, to
ensure that the Strategic Management Plan (SMP) includes a description of the key
business transformation challenges to be addressed, sufficient context for why specific
goals and strategies were chosen, and measures to address core activities. (See
page 25/GAO Draft Report.)

DoD RESPONSE: Partially concur. Future releases of the SMP will include key
business transformation challenges, context for the inclusion of specific goals and
strategies, and measures to address core activities. However, in crafting the SMP and
executing its performance management system, the Department's senior leaders will
continue to make strategic choices about which broad goals are most important and,
within those goals, on which initiatives and key indicators they will focus their
management attention.

RECOMMENDATION 2: The GAO recommends that the Secretary of Defense direct
the Deputy Secretary of Defense, in his capacity as the Chief Management Officer, to
further define DoD's performance management approach, by outlining elements such as
how it will consider the various sources of performance information along with SMP
performance results to monitor progress in achieving business goals and identify
corrective actions and ensure this information is reviewed on a regular basis. (See
page 25/GAO Draft Report.)

DoD RESPONSE: Concur. The Department will continue to improve and
institutionalize operations of the Defense Business Council (DBC) to provide unified
direction and leadership to efficiently and effectively manage the DoD business mission
area. By charter, the DBC integrates and reviews performance information to track
progress against strategic goals and hold Department leaders accountable for results.
Issues will continue to be raised to the Deputy's Management Action Group (DMAG),
the mechanism created by the Deputy Secretary of Defense for executing a common
management approach across the disparate topics and processes of the Department.

Appendix IV: GAO Contact and Staff Acknowledgments

GAO Contact	Sharon L. Pickup, (202)-512-9619 or pickups@gao.gov
Acknowledgments	In addition to the contact named above, James A. Reynolds, Assistant Director; Gabrielle A. Carrington; Laurie Choi; Grace Coleman; Aimee Elivert; Michael Silver; and Nicole Willems made key contributions to this report.

GAO's Mission	The Government Accountability Office, the audit, evaluation, and investigative arm of Congress, exists to support Congress in meeting its constitutional responsibilities and to help improve the performance and accountability of the federal government for the American people. GAO examines the use of public funds; evaluates federal programs and policies; and provides analyses, recommendations, and other assistance to help Congress make informed oversight, policy, and funding decisions. GAO's commitment to good government is reflected in its core values of accountability, integrity, and reliability.
Obtaining Copies of GAO Reports and Testimony	The fastest and easiest way to obtain copies of GAO documents at no cost is through GAO's website (http://www.gao.gov). Each weekday afternoon, GAO posts on its website newly released reports, testimony, and correspondence. To have GAO e-mail you a list of newly posted products, go to http://www.gao.gov and select "E-mail Updates."
Order by Phone	The price of each GAO publication reflects GAO's actual cost of production and distribution and depends on the number of pages in the publication and whether the publication is printed in color or black and white. Pricing and ordering information is posted on GAO's website, http://www.gao.gov/ordering.htm. Place orders by calling (202) 512-6000, toll free (866) 801-7077, or TDD (202) 512-2537. Orders may be paid for using American Express, Discover Card, MasterCard, Visa, check, or money order. Call for additional information.
Connect with GAO	Connect with GAO on Facebook, Flickr, Twitter, and YouTube. Subscribe to our RSS Feeds or E-mail Updates. Listen to our Podcasts. Visit GAO on the web at www.gao.gov.
To Report Fraud, Waste, and Abuse in Federal Programs	Contact: Website: http://www.gao.gov/fraudnet/fraudnet.htm E-mail: fraudnet@gao.gov Automated answering system: (800) 424-5454 or (202) 512-7470
Congressional Relations	Katherine Siggerud, Managing Director, siggerudk@gao.gov, (202) 512-4400, U.S. Government Accountability Office, 441 G Street NW, Room 7125, Washington, DC 20548
Public Affairs	Chuck Young, Managing Director, youngc1@gao.gov, (202) 512-4800 U.S. Government Accountability Office, 441 G Street NW, Room 7149 Washington, DC 20548

Please Print on Recycled Paper.